Dear Suicide

By Aaron Fields

Copyright © 2020 Aaron Fields. All rights reserved.

Published by The Write Perspective, LLC

Dallas, Texas,

All rights reserved. No part of this book shall be reproduced or transmitted in any form or by any means, electronic, mechanical, magnetic, photographic, including photocopying, recording or by any information storage and retrieval system, without the prior written permission of the publisher. No copyright liability is assumed with respect to the use of the information contained in this book. Even though every precaution has been taken in preparation for this book, the publisher/author assumes no responsibility for errors or omissions. Neither is any liability assumed for any damage that results from the use of the information in this book.

ISBN: 978-1-953962-52-2

CONTENTS

Chapter 1 Suicidal..1

Chapter 2 Assume The Responsibility..3

Chapter 3 Don't Leave The Person Alone..4

Chapter 4 Don't Keep It A Secret...5

Chapter 5 Never Dare Them To Commit Suicide..............................7

Chapter 6 Be An Active Listener & Acknowledge Feelings............................9

Chapter 7 Alternatives To Suicide.................................... 11

Chapter 8 Seek Help..13

Chapter 9 Ask Your Friend If He Or She Has Any Goals...............16

Chapter 10 Addressing Your Own Needs...20

Chapter 11 Reflection.. 23

Notes...

Something To Think About Before You Read

"Don't Self-Destruct,"

----------Aaron Fields

Word from the Author

Before an individual develops a strategy to help others, he or she must learn how to help themselves. Although this book will discuss multiple ways on how to help someone that is suicidal, always remember to never neglect your own needs. Regardless of what you might be enduring in your life, if you are thinking of taking your own life, understand that there are ways to get through the pain and address the emotions. All you need is time, support, and a healthy mind, preferably a spiritual mindset.

If a suicidal thought has ever come across your mind before, don't feel bad and kill yourself over it (no pun intended). Many people in this world have thought about taking their own lives away during a time when they've felt lost and powerless. Luckily, faith and hope can always be replenished. Whatever circumstances you are in right now; it's only temporary and not permanent. If you think you're brought into this world by mistake, you are wrong, because everything in life happens for a reason. Before you even contemplate about taking away your own life, think of the people who depend on you, think about the people you can brighten up with your presence, and remember the moments that will remind you how special life is. It takes courage, strength, and a great deal of mental fortitude to face the hardships of life.

I will never force you to decide, but I implore you to value your life. Yes, I understand your emotions are constantly changing, but how you feel today may not be the same as how you'll feel tomorrow or next month. The reason I emphasize the importance of valuing your life is because taking your own life away will create grief and distress in the lives of your friends and family. Remember, there are many things for you to accomplish in this world, so don't waste it by ending your life early. We all have to die eventually, so make the most out of your life while you're still here.

1

SUICIDAL

Dear You,

It may be difficult to fathom why someone you care about would contemplate suicide, yet for some, life can be unbearable. Your friend or loved one may have lost hope of things getting better and may wish to end their life by any means necessary. Whatever the reason might be, it's never worth killing yourself.

With a person who is suicidal, always pay attention to his/her behavior. If someone close to you is giving away meaningful possessions, expressing interest in obtaining a dangerous weapon, or writing or posting about death or helplessness, pay attention. It's crucial to recognize the severe signs of a suicidal person. Signs like depression, anxiety, neglect of physical and mental health, excessive drinking, and drug usage.

One of the most frightening experiences an individual can have is hearing a person they care about say they want to die. Don't dismiss these warning signs as attention-seeking behavior; it's important to take them seriously. If you are not sure what to do or how to help, at least start off by asking them direct questions, especially if you're worried. Although, I know some people may be hesitant to ask, as they believe it could make matters worse. If this is you, speak to a professional or a person who is trustworthy and equipped to handle the situation. Whatever you do, taking action is always better than not doing anything at all. Here are a few more suggestions to think about for helping someone that is suicidal.

2

ASSUME THE RESPONSIBILITY

"Someone has to do it,"

Lack of support and awareness for the victim leads to the failure to save suicidal individuals. Even though people can tell when someone is suicidal, they still won't do anything because they assume someone else will help. Yes, I understand it's possible that you're busy with your own life and you may not want to get involved. It's also possible that you may not care enough about the issue. After all, it's much easier to say, "It's not my problem." Imagine a world with every person assuming someone else will take care of the situation. How much would we accomplish?

It's essential to take up the responsibility, but also crucial to realize that you can't save everyone. If someone is rejecting your offer of assistance, it's likely they don't want to get help. Even though your intentions are good, don't fixate on the fact that your help is not being appreciated.

Accepting the fact that you can't always stop someone from taking their own life away is essential, as everyone has autonomy over their decisions. In life, you are ultimately responsible for yourself. If you help people along the way, good for you; however, you are not a superhero. While it's nice to help others, it's not your job to save the world.

3

DON'T LEAVE THE PERSON ALONE

"Being alone is not always safe."

If you know someone who is at high risk of suicide, do not leave them alone until help arrives. You should never take that person as a joke if they've expressed suicidal thoughts or talked about creating a plan to take their life away. Give him or her respect and take them seriously.

As you stay with the victim, try to keep the conversation going by asking direct questions about his or her feelings. If possible, get a trusted individual to stay with them until more help arrives. If possible, take note of any signs and remove any drugs, alcohol, sharp objects, or firearms that could be used for a suicide attempt. However, if all else fails and you're desperate; call 911or a trusted individual. Should it be necessary, get the individual to a hospital immediately.

A person in a suicidal state may not think logically because of the depths of their depression, leading them to feel hopeless. The reason you can't leave a suicidal person alone is because you and the rest of the world are created to have relationships and connections with other people. A person suffering from suicidal thoughts is disconnected from the world. Neglecting to offer them help or resources will only make matters worse. The key component to helping a suicidal friend is to start off by showing a genuine interest in helping that person.

DON'T KEEP IT A SECRET

"Not all secrets are worth keeping."

Don't make a promise to keep their suicidal thoughts a secret if you suspect your friend or loved one is suicidal. Yes, it's important to be understanding, but it's more important for you to explain to them you can't keep their suicidal thoughts a secret. Don't worry about risking a friendship, especially if their life is in danger. You'll be better off losing a relationship from violating a secret than going to their funeral. Who knows? That person may come back one day and thank you for saving their life. If by any chance you don't see yourself as the right person for the job, ask for help and never try to help a suicidal person by yourself.

Keep in mind that the price for keeping someone's suicidal thoughts "a secret" might be the death of that person. It's safe to assume that people who are suicidal are experiencing emotional pain. As it pertains to their mental health, it is not your job to assess the victim, leave that to the mental health providers. You can, however, offer support and advice, which is just as important. When a person says they want to commit suicide, most likely they are not thinking logically and they're not being themselves. Remember, even though they are not thinking clearly, the emotions are real.

Instead of keeping things a secret, let the suicidal person know that it's okay to talk to someone. In most cases, they will bottle up their feelings because they feel ashamed. Most of these individuals have never talked about their suicidal thoughts with anyone. This can cause them to become isolated in their own thoughts, believing that no one is there for them, when, in reality, nobody is aware of their circumstances.

5

NEVER DARE THEM TO COMMIT SUICIDE

"Never encourage someone to do something that you're not willing to do."

One of the worst things you can do to an individual is encourage him or her to commit suicide. Not only is it a terrible insult, but it's also dangerous, especially if the person is already depressed and mentally sick. If I'm being honest, encouraging someone to commit suicide says much more about the person saying it than the recipient.

Instead of treating the individual with disdain, let the person know you care by voicing your concerns. Ask what is troubling them. If you by any chance feel reluctant to help them, try looking at the bigger picture of the current situation rather than just yourself. Always reassure your friend that he or she is not alone and explain to them you can help them solve their problems. Explain to them that emotional pain is temporary, and suicide is permanent.

Instead of bringing in additional pain and suffering to the individual, add value to their life by holding them in the highest regard. When you show value in a person, it means you appreciate them as a human being. Let's be honest, when someone is special to you, you won't allow him or her to kill themselves without giving it a fight. You'll probably do more than expected to make sure the person knows their value to you. After all, you don't want to live with the regret of wondering if you could have prevented the suicide.

6

BE AN ACTIVE LISTENER & ACKNOWLEDGE FEELINGS

"Listen before you speak."

One of the most important things for a suicidal person to have in the middle of a crisis is an active listener. When you listen to and question a suicidal person, it demonstrates that you are open to discussing anything with them, including their feelings. Understand that emotions are real, so not respecting how the person may feel can shut down your communication with them.

Active listening is acknowledging the person's feelings and understanding the message they convey. The more you listen to a person, the more validated he or she feels, which can ultimately create a sense of closeness. To show a better understanding of what the individual is trying to say to you, pay close attention to their words and repeat any ideas or phrases they deliver to you. This will confirm to them they are being listened to and understood.

Believe it or not, you can get more out of life by spending more time listening than talking. When you actively listen to your suicidal friend, refrain from yelling or interrupting. It's possible that the friend is frightened and confused, so screaming and cutting them off will not make their thoughts less troublesome. The more you facilitate active listening; the better off you'll be in supporting your suicidal friend in whatever it is they're going through.

When it comes to active listening, do not dismiss what the suicidal person shares with you. Even if you have a brilliant solution to their problem, wait until they make their point and then take the time to weigh out your thoughts. As you voice your concerns, it's always important to ask yourself if you're being helpful in the conversation, or are you making this situation about you. It's okay to step out of your comfort zone by awaiting your turn and approaching the situation with sincerity.

7

ALTERNATIVES TO SUICIDE

"It's okay to have options."

Mental illness turns all thoughts, opinions, and emotions away from anything positive. For some, suicide seems like the only way to escape the pain. Mental illness can make you think, see, hear, and even believe things that aren't exactly how they really are. It's as if there's a negative force surrounding your mind.

If your depression is taking over, understand that it doesn't have to be that way forever. There are many alternatives to suicide, and the best part is that the other options will keep you alive on this planet much longer. Just because your friend or loved one's depression is making them contemplate suicide, it doesn't mean you have to allow their thoughts to manifest into an actual suicide attempt.

Your friend needs to understand that suicide is permanent, not the solution to a problem. Once you kill yourself, there is no more living. Encourage your friend to follow a path to healing. Let him or her know they don't have to die. You may discover that the victim has no genuine desire to commit suicide. It's always worth seeking help even if your friend no longer desires to end their life, as you never know what might happen.

Life is satisfying when you can be supportive and authentic with the other person about their experiences. Always let your friend know depressed feelings can change overtime. Help him or her explore different solutions to their problems. If the path they've been on is not keeping them safe, it may be time for them to find a new one. Although everyone may have a distinct set of beliefs and values, believing in something bigger than yourself can always give you a reason to keep living.

8

SEEK HELP

"You can't do everything on your own,"

Most likely, your suicidal friend opened up to you because they trust you and have confidence in you. Encourage them to trust your decision to seek professional support. Most suicidal victims don't realize that depression can be treatable, and as a result, they never reach out for help. With you by their side, they may be more likely to seek help. If your friend gets mad at you for helping them, oh well. It's much better to have an angry friend than a dead one.

It may be hard for you to get your friend to discuss their feelings to someone other than you. It's possible that their friends and family may not fully understand why they have these suicidal thoughts. Give them confidence to reach out to the people that care about them and will help. If I were you, I wouldn't hesitate to get them help from a place of worship, or a community support group. Sometimes all a person needs is to feel connected and supported by someone.

Other than depression, there are other issues that can lead to suicide as well. One thing that life stressors have in common is that they can make any individual feel hopeless. Most people who are suicidal can't seem to understand that seeking support can help them regain a much greater perspective on their life. As long as they take one step at a time and don't act impulsively, life will get much better for them. In life, you can never go wrong with rational thinking.

Let's Talk About It

Everyone experiences hardships in life, but many don't know how to manage it. When major life stressors come up, it's important that you know how to handle them properly to avoid depression and suicidal thinking. Tell me about some life stressors you are dealing with and how you are handling them.

_____
_____
_____
_____
_____
_____
_____
_____
_____
_____
_____
_____
_____

9

ASK YOUR FRIEND IF HE OR SHE HAVE ANY GOALS

"When a person doesn't know where to go, most likely they won't know how to get there."

Yes, suicide is a heavy topic to face, but the truth about suicide is that it's not handled as well as it should be, and as a result, many lives are lost. To develop a better understanding about suicide, it's important to know where the thoughts come from. Do you know anyone who has committed suicide or at least thought about it? If so, can you recall the feelings you experienced when you found out?

_____

_____

_____

_____

_____

_____

_____

_____

_____

Whether it was your friend, neighbor, or relative that took their own life away, it all leaves us with feelings of sadness and confusion. What would drive a person to such depths of despairs that they would want to commit suicide? Is throwing away everything the answer? Keep in mind the individual will leave everyone behind, including friends, family, children, and their spouse. Could it be possible that most people who commit suicide never established a vision for their life (**let this sink in for a few minutes**)?

Although there are multiple factors that play a role in a person wanting to commit suicide, we all need to understand the heaviness of the mind. Most of the time, people who are suicidal don't have a purpose in life. When a person has no hope for their future, there is no self-control. As their friend, it's important for you to help them develop a clearer vision by encouraging them to live a much more focused life. Sometimes finding a purpose in life can simplify everything else.

The first thing your friend/relative needs from you is to help them identify what matters in their life. If he or she doesn't have an answer to what matters in their lives right now, that's all right. However, it's important to at least brainstorm and work towards that idea. Whatever your friend wants to do in life, there are resources out there to support their experiences. All they need to do is craft their vision statement and describe what their ideal life looks like.

My Vision Statement: For each section, answer the question to the best of your ability. In order to have a fulfilled life, one must think about the things he/she wants to experience.

Health- how do you feel physically, mentally, and spiritually? _____

_____

_____

_____

Skills- what are your abilities and what do you need to maximize them?_____

_____

_____

Time- how will you use your time to fulfill your vision?_____

_____

_____

_____

Attitude- how will you use your outlook on life to grow and improve as a human being?_____

_____

_____

_____

Relationships- who are you surrounding yourself with and are they contributing positively to your life? _____

_____

_____

_____

Character Development- what are some of your admirable traits you love about yourself? Are you content with the person you are? _____

_____

_____

_____

_____

_____

10

ADDRESSING YOUR OWN NEEDS

"NEVER NEGLECT YOURSELF,"

It's okay to admit when you're tired. Being in a helpful role for a suicidal friend is exhausting physically, emotionally, mentally, and even spiritually. Be sure to address your own needs during these circumstances because not putting yourself as a priority is going to be a major problem.

Talk to someone or seek counseling to address your situation. Don't allow anyone to make you feel selfish about wanting to take care of yourself. Treating yourself with love, compassion, and respect is an indicator of self-worth. As you continue to nurture your inner being, you'll be able to give more of yourself to others.

Addressing your needs and taking care of yourself is essential for your health and well-being. Most people find that their physical, mental, and spiritual health is all connected to each other. In order to stay well, one must learn how to take care of every aspect of their life. The importance of incorporating a healthy mind and spirit into your life has many implications in developing a resilient attitude.

Taking the time to check in with yourself allows you the opportunity to evaluate where you are in your life. You may find that you need to readjust your way of thinking and try different coping strategies to solve your personal and interpersonal issues. If you have experienced low points in your life, you understand how difficult it can be to move on.

Have you ever considered using a journal? Not only having a journal will help you learn more about yourself, it can also help with regulating your emotions. The operative word is "regulate". Usually, when people make poor decisions, they realize they are acting on emotion instead of logic. Yes, emotions can play a major role in anyone's decision making because anxiety, anger, and sadness in one area of your life can spill over into other areas. Acknowledge your emotions and always pay attention to the way you're feeling. Understand how your emotions can disrupt your way of thinking and how it influences your behavior. Sometimes in life, all you need are just the facts to help you think more rationally about your options to make better choices. The best part about thinking logically is that it can prevent any emotions from getting the best of you.

Whatever goal you work on, always be clear about your purpose and how your life will be different once you achieve it. It also wouldn't hurt for you to consider using the skills you possess that will help you accomplish your goals. Seek resources and a strong support system that can help you get through the process. As long as you continue to stay focused on improving your life outcomes, you'll be one step closer to making something out of yourself.

Ways to Address Your Needs

Healthy Living: avoid drugs and excess alcohol, get some rest, eat healthy, exercise, and get regular medical check-ups

Surround yourself with good people: develop a sense of belonging and consider joining a group of people that will always bring out the best in you while also holding you accountable.

Hygiene: For psychological, social, medical, and personal reasons, practicing good hygiene is essential for your health. The more you take care of yourself, the more likely it is for you to improve the way you view yourself.

When it comes to addressing your needs, what are some hobbies/activities you try to implement every day?

_____

_____

_____

_____

_____

_____

_____

_____

_____

11

REFLECTION

"Find meaning in your experiences,"

Although this book pertains to someone you know that is suicidal, this book applies to you too. A person without a purpose develops a meaningless life. Lacking purpose in your life creates a lot of uncertainty. Doubt will crawl inside of you and take root within your spirit. If you're not careful, it will make your life feel empty inside.

You could have everything you ever wanted: a spouse, a wonderful house, beautiful children, all the money in the world. However, if you have no purpose in life, it won't mean anything to you. I don't believe anti-depression pills will help you solve your problems. However, I believe that understanding the reason for your existence in this world will help you.

Believe it or not, many people have lived several years of their lives with suicidal thoughts. The goal is for you to help others, including yourself, that are in danger of falling victim to these dark thoughts. Many people have lived it, but very few escaped it. Can you?

Understand that you are here for a specific reason. Not only are you unique, but no one can ever be you. Why? It's because you comprise your very own ideas, skills, and talents. You are not alone on this journey; there is someone out there that cares about you. Don't allow depression, anger, and hopelessness to take over your frame of mind. Just because there are trials and tribulations doesn't mean there's no hope. Your life matters too, and once you understand the gifts and talents you possess; you'll know your worth.

Suicide is never the answer to solving your problems. If you or anyone you know is having suicidal thoughts, reach out to a trusted individual that can help you. It's time to transform your suicidal thinking into thoughts of optimism. Yes, mental illness can take a huge toll on your well-being, but overcoming your struggles can bring you closer to understanding the meaning of your life. Thus, you will have something to live for.

If you have the opportunity to learn from another person's experiences, take it. It's easy to think you're the only one that has terrible life experiences and can't relate to anyone. Sometimes taking a moment to step back and hear about other people's stories can help you realize that the world is a lot smaller than you think. Looking into the lives of others and how they managed their hardships can give you knowledge and understanding, which can benefit your life.

Remember, there is always hope. If you don't like your current situation in life, you always have to look on the bright side. Take into consideration that there are people with far worse circumstances than you. Poor decisions, a challenging upbringing, or unfortunate luck have caused many of them to contemplate a life of crime. If you don't like the condition that you're in, keep in mind that there's always a way out, and killing yourself is not one of them. When you have a moment to yourself, start contemplating on the things you want to do with your life. What are you gifted at? Where do you want to go? What brings a smile to your face? What motivates you to stay positive?

It's inevitable that you're going to reach a low point and hit a few bumps on the road. It's easy to feel unnoticed, and it's easy to feel like you're a burden to everyone. In reality, that's not the case because no one is perfect and everyone makes mistakes. So give life a chance, have hope, have faith, find your purpose in life, and always remember that there is someone out there who loves you.

Sincerely,
Aaron Fields

NOTES